ii. Horizontal mobility among teachers from lower-class to middle-class schools
iii. Self-fulfilling prophecy identifying academic achievement with social class

PROBLEMS WITH CHANGE
1. School bureaucracy difficult to change
2. Schools function to pass on norms and values, thus are conservative in nature
3. Lack of financial resources for lasting change
4. School boards dominated by white, upper-middle class professionals who want to maintain status quo
5. Predictability and standardization of curriculum
6. Hire teachers compatible with administrative ideals
7. Local officials cannot instigate change because policies determined at state/federal level

CHARACTERISTICS OF AMERICAN EDUCATION
1. **Mass education**: 40% Americans go on to higher education versus 10% Western European
2. **Pragmatic orientation**: Education purposes to educate people for democracy
3. **Decentralization and community control**: In the United States, education is decentralized
4. **Formal structure of the school**: Bureaucratic form of organization
5. **Higher education**: College degree often essential for success in modern world

CURRENT ISSUES IN AMERICAN EDUCATION
1. **Discipline and violence**: "Question Authority" is slogan for 21st century
2. Effectiveness
   a. **Problem**: Denouncing organizations is an American pastime, "rising tide of mediocrity" (NCEE report, 1983)
   b. **Solutions**: Child's social background most important (**Coleman**, et al., 1966)
3. **Race, class, education**: Social conditions do not promote community segregation

FAMILY

Procreation and affection

"FUNCTIONS" OF FAMILY
1. Regulation of sexual behavior
2. Socialization of children
3. Care and emotional support
4. Maintaining economic system
5. Conferring social status upon its members

VARIATIONS IN FAMILY FORM
1. **Nuclear family:** Married couple and dependent children
2. **Extended family**: Nuclear family and relations (e.g. grandparents)
3. **Single-parent households**
4. **Monogamy**: Marriage between two people
5. **Polygamy**: Having more than one marriage partner
   a. **Polygyny**: One man/two or more women
   b. **Polyandry**: One woman/more than one man

MATE SELECTION
1. Romantic love is relatively modern concept
2. Rules of selection
   a. **Exogamy**: Marriage outside cultural group
   b. **Endogamy**: Marriage within ethnic, religious or economic group
   c. **Homogamy**: Mate of similar background
   d. **Heterogamy**: Mate of different background
3. **Egalitarianism**: Relationships characterized by lack of power differentials between husbands and wives and between parents and children
4. **Patterns of descent**
   a. **Unilineal descent**: Traces descent through one family line
   b. **Patrilineal descent**: Traces through male line
   c. **Matrilineal descent**: Traces through female line
   d. **Non-unilineal descent**: Traces through both lines
5. **Patterns of residence**: Where new families establish residence
6. Patterns of authority
   a. **Patriarchy**: Family authority vested in male
   b. **Matriarchy**: Family authority vested in female
   c. **Egalitarian**: Family authority vested in both

ANALYSIS OF THE FAMILY
1. **Universal functions of family**: Functionalist view
   a. Regulation of sexual activity
   b. Replacement of societal members
   c. Socialization
   d. Social placement
   e. Intimacy and companionship
2. **Dysfunctions of the family**: Conflict perspective
   a. Subordination of women
   b. Violence in the family
   c. Perpetuates stratification system
   d. Delegitimizes variant lifestyles

THE CONTEMPORARY AMERICAN FAMILY
1. Monogamous, select partner by individual choice, bilateral descent system, egalitarian authority systems, share socialization with institutions and organizations
2. Consider romantic love to be essential for marriage
3. Majority of married couples desire children
4. Dual-earner families
5. Increasing amount of family violence
6. Marital dissolution/reconstituted families

FAMILY CYCLE
1. Prechildren - increasingly, couples choose to remain childless
2. Parenthood
3. Empty nest

PROBLEMS
1. **Violence**
   a. Primarily directed against women and children
   b. Societal problems - American way of life
   c. Intensity of family life makes family particularly vulnerable to violence
2. **Divorce**
   a. Rapid increase in past two decades
   b. More options are now available to woman
   c. Increased tolerance of divorce

RELIGION

High morality

UNDERSTANDING BELIEF SYSTEM
1. **Emile Durkheim**
   a. Religion acts to hold a society together
   b. Objects are given a sacred meaning by society; objects are not intrinsically sacred
2. **Max Weber**
   a. Link between religious and economic institutions
   b. Religion reflects beliefs about economic success
3. **Karl Marx**
   a. Religion promotes the status quo
   b. Religion acts as "opiate" of masses that encourages them to ignore their economic plight

VARIETIES
1. **Theism**: Belief in powerful super being
   a. **Monotheism**: Belief in one god
   b. **Polytheism**: Belief in many gods
2. The **church** (organized religion)
   a. Compliments values of dominant society
   b. **Hierarchy of authority**: Professional leadership
   c. Members usually born into faith
3. **Sects and Cults**
   a. Contrary to dominant society
   b. Little formal training of leadership, often based on charismatic qualities of person
   c. Members enter sect through adult conversions

RELIGIOUS TRENDS IN U.S.
1. **Civil religion**
   a. Mix of American nationalism and Judeo-Christian religion in secular activities, e.g. baseball games, high school graduations
   b. U.S. monitors world's moral and ethical behavior
2. **Importance of religion**
   a. Fewer see religion as significant force in their lives
   b. Church attendance has decreased
   c. Intermarriage between religions has increased
3. **Decline in membership** and significance of traditional religions
4. **Rise in Christian fundamentalism**
   a. Reliance on literal words in the Bible
   b. Politically conservative and resentful of change
   c. Use of television to carry their message
   d. Often evangelical (belief in a personal relationship with Jesus Christ)

FUNCTIONS OF RELIGION
1. Social cohesion
2. Providing meaning in life
3. **Social concerns**: Society's norms based on set of religious beliefs
4. Psychological support
5. Secular ideologies viewed as secular religions, e.g. fascism, humanism

MAJOR WORLD RELIGIONS
1. **Christianity**: One billion followers, 20% of world population
2. **Islam**: 500 million followers
3. **Hinduism**: 500 million followers
4. **Buddhism**: 250 million followers
5. **Confucianism**: 150 million followers
6. **Judaism**: 17 million followers

RELIGION IN THE UNITED STATES
1. **Religious affiliation**: 70% belong to a particular religious organization; 65% Protestant, 24% Catholic
2. **Religiosity**: Importance of religion in life of individual and society

CORRELATES OF RELIGIOUS AFFILIATION
1. **Social class**: Relationship between religion and social class
2. **Ethnicity and race**: Internal racial and ethnic diversity in religious groups
3. **Political attitudes**: Religion influences but does not determine these
4. **Religious revival**: Decline in religious affiliation over past 20 years

Editor: **Wayne Mayhall** U.S.$4.95

Customer Hotline # 1.800.230.9522

NOTE TO STUDENT: This **QUICKSTUDY**® guide is **an annotated outline of the major topics** taught in introductory Sociology courses. Due to its condensed format, use it as a Sociology guide, but not as a replacement for assigned class work.

ISBN-13: 978-157222647-0
ISBN-10: 157222647-1
50495
9 781572 226470
6 54614 20647 3

BarCharts, Inc.® WORLD'S #1 ACADEMIC OUTLINE
Quick Study® ACADEMIC

SOCIOLOGY

THE BASIC PRINCIPLES OF SOCIOLOGY FOR INTRODUCTORY COURSES

INTRODUCTION

SOCIOLOGICAL PERSPECTIVE

SOCIAL SCIENCES

Sociology is the scientific study of human social behavior and human association, and results of social activities

1. **C. Wright Mills** (1959)
   a. Individuals belong to groups; sociology focuses on social forces, "the sociological imagination"
   b. **Utility perspective:** Individuals understand the general by abstracting specific
2. Groups influence our behavior; **Emile Durkheim's** suicide studies show suicide as function of social integration
3. Groups take on characteristics independent of their members, i.e., the whole is > sum of its parts
4. Sociologists focus on behavior patterns of groups, i.e., differences based on sex, race, age, class, etc.

SOCIOLOGY & SCIENCE

Sociology is the scientific study of social behavior and arrangements

1. Assumptions of science
   a. We discover laws of nature, not create them
   b. There is order in nature
   c. Science assumes an orderly world of cause and effect
2. Tools of science
   a. **Theories**: Explanation of how two or more phenomenon relate
   b. **Hypothesis**: Variables of theories form "educated guess"
   c. **Data**: Observable information, such as facts and statistics
3. Sociology as science
   a. Sociology constructs theories to explain social life
   b. Sociological study lacks precision of other sciences
   c. Sociology surpasses level of common sense to rigorous study

FOUNDERS OF SOCIOLOGY

INFLUENCED BY THE INDUSTRIAL REVOLUTION

AUGUST COMTE, 1798-1857
1. Belief - need to understand society as it was, rather than what ought to be
2. Positivism - path to understanding world based on science
3. Used "sociology" - Greek/Latin: Study of society

HERBERT SPENCER, 1820-1903
1. **SOCIAL DARWINISM:** Survival of the Fittest - most intelligent, ambitious people rise to top
2. Most of his work has been discredited

KARL MARX, 1818-1883
1. The means of production/economic sector is most important in any society
2. Historical change occurs through class conflict between owners and workers

EMILE DURKHEIM, 1855-1917
1. Bonds/functions hold society together (social integration)
2. Society is held together by **mechanical solidarity** (a social/moral consensus) and by **organic solidarity** (a dependency of roles among people)

MAX WEBER, 1864-1920
1. *Verstehen* or insight is important to understanding behavior
2. Religion powerful in creating economic system
3. Rationality more pervasive through development of bureaucratic structures

GEORGE SIMMEL, 1858-1918
1. Rejected the organic analogy of Spencer
2. Society is an "intricate web of multiple relations between individuals who are in constant interaction with one another"
3. **"Formal sociology"**: Led to research into "social types"

CURRENT APPROACHES

MACROSOCIOLOGY [TOTALITY OF SOCIETY]
1. **Structural functionalism**
   a. All society's parts are interdependent and function as an organism
   b. Society very stable and change occurs gradually
   c. Consensus among members on norms and values
   d. Key proponents: **Talcott Parsons**, **Robert Merton**
2. **Conflict Theory**
   a. Parts exist in tension/competition with each other
   b. Constant change and conflict due to inequality among different groups
   c. Disagreement over distribution of power/resources
   d. Key proponents: **Lewis Coser**, **Ralf Dahrendorf**

MICROSOCIOLOGY [SMALL GROUP BEHAVIOR]
1. Symbolic Interaction
   a. Society is based on the ongoing interaction between people
   b. Attach meanings to behavior, and actions and reactions influence behavior
   c. Key proponents: **Herbert Blumer**, **Erving Goffman**
   d. Focus on identity issues, particularly the sense of self, which is a social product

ETHNOMETHODOLOGY
1. Study processes by which meanings are created and shared
2. There is no ordered social world unless participants agree upon it
3. Key proponents: **Alfred Schutz** and **Harold Garfinkel**

EXCHANGE THEORY
1. Social life is a process of bargaining and negotiation
2. Interaction proceeds on a cost/benefit analysis
3. Theory introduced by **George Homans** in 1950

RESEARCH METHODS

SELECT TOPIC
1. **Methodology:** Directs sociological investigations and provides a way to verify results
2. Review literature already researched
3. Select specific variables to be studied
   a. **Independent variable**: Influences dependent variables - cause, e.g. sex, age, race
   b. **Dependent variable**: Influenced by independent variables - effect, e.g. topic studied
4. Experiments
   a. **Laboratory experiments**: Results may not work in "real" world
   b. **Field experiments**: Study people in real-life situations
   c. **Experimental Method**: Experimental Group (exposed to variable) versus Control Group (not exposed to variable)
   d. **"Hawthorne Effect"**: Research influenced by perception of subjects
5. Formulate hypothesis using variables
6. Correlation
   a. **Positive**: If two values increase/decrease simultaneously
   b. **Negative**: One value increases/decreases, the other value does not
7. Establishing cause and effect
   a. **Spurious correlation**: Just coincidental
   b. **Controls**: Techniques to eliminate confusing factors
8. Interconnection of theory and research
   a. Theory and research go hand-in-hand
   b. Sociological theory is useless without research

THE RESEARCH PROCESS
1. **Step One:** Defining the problem to study
2. **Step Two:** Reviewing the literature
3. **Step Three:** Formulating hypothesis (an explicit statement about relationship between variables)
4. **Step Four:** Considering the ethical issues involved
5. **Step Five:** Choosing a research design
   a. **Survey**: Sample population questioned; **Sampling**: Small cross-section of population for study; **Questionnaire**: Series of questions to respond to for study
   b. **Interviews**: Conversations (researcher/subject)
   c. **Observation**: Enter field of subject as participant or observer
      i. detached observation – researcher remains outside what is being observed
      ii. participant observation – researcher is active participant in study
   d. **Experiments**: Variables are controlled
   e. **Secondary analysis**: Using data already collected
6. **Step Six**: Collect & analyze data
   a. Use appropriate statistical measures
   b. Conclusions must withstand scrutiny
   c. Original hypothesis confirmed, refuted, or modified
7. **Step Seven**: Drawing conclusions, researcher can add new knowledge, challenge validity or modify previous knowledge, and raise new questions

PROBLEMS IN DOING RESEARCH
1. **Technical difficulties**
   a. **Reliability**: Consistency in study methods and results
   b. **Validity**: Measuring what is claimed to be measured
2. **Practical difficulties**
   a. **Cooperation**: Subjects must view research as important
   b. **Behavior changes**: Self-awareness may result in alteration
   c. **Ethical concerns**: To what extent do people have a right to decide if they should be studied?

SOCIAL STRUCTURE

RELATIONSHIPS & INDIVIDUAL

CULTURE

Shared beliefs, behaviors

WHAT IS CULTURE?
1. **Human invention**: We create culture and are made human by it
2. **Limitations**: Culture restricts human freedom, restrains unevenly
3. **Expectations**: Culture enhances freedom, takes us beyond instinct

COMPONENTS
1. **Material culture**: All tangible, concrete creations of society
2. **Nonmaterial culture**: Abstract creations of society that are transmitted across generations
   a. **Symbols**: Objects with agreed-upon meaning
   b. **Signs**: Representations that stand for something else
   c. **Language**: Most important system of symbols
      • **Sapir-Whorf****(next page): Language influences perception
   d. **Gestures**: Movements of body with socially agreed-upon meanings
   e. **Values**: Central beliefs about acceptable or unacceptable, good or bad, desirable or undesirable
   f. Dominant American values

i. Superiority over nature
ii. Equality of opportunity
iii. Achievement and success
iv. Individualism
3. **Norms**: Agreed-upon behaviors on how to act
   a. **Mores**: Behaviors that deal with moral standards (e.g. stealing, cheating, lying)
   b. **Folkways**: Less significant (e.g. not wearing tie to opera)
   c. **Laws**: Norms established and enforced by the political authority of the society
4. **Knowledge and beliefs**: Knowledge is those conclusions based on some measure of empirical evidence; belief is those conclusions without sufficient empirical support

Linguistic Relativity Hypothesis
1. The nature of language affects our perception of the world
2. Language directs society's attention to certain features
3. Formulated by **Edward Sapir** (1929) and **Lee Whorf** (1956)

"IDEAL" & "REAL" CULTURE
1. Norms structure behavior by defining culturally approved modes of action
2. People do not always behave as expected
3. Norms should not be confused with behavior

CULTURAL DIVERSITY
1. Diversity between societies
   a. Societies differ in values and norms
   b. Diversity demonstrates variability and flexibility of human arrangements
2. Diversity within a society
   a. **Subculture**: Group with a distinctive lifestyle within a society
   b. **Counterculture**: Group with behavior contrary to the dominant culture
3. **Cultural relativism**: No cultural practice is inherently good or bad; each understood in terms of its place in larger cultural configuration
4. **Ethnocentrism**: Opposite of cultural relativism, the tendency to view one's own culture as morally superior to others and to judge other cultures by the standards of one's own

AMERICAN CULTURAL THEMES
Robin Williams (1970), a limited number of basic American cultural values
1. Americans place emphasis on achievement and success
2. Are highly competitive and measure self-worth by success
3. Activity, work and occupational activities are emphasized
4. Especially value efficiency and practicality (**Taylor**, 1911), "time and management studies"; pragmatism is American philosophical system
5. Have a strong humanitarian side and cherish freedom and democracy
6. Think in terms of social categories, which sometimes leads to racism and group superiority

CULTURE & SOCIOBIOLOGY
Edward Wilson (1975) introduced "sociobiology," the systematic study of the biological basis of human behavior
1. Predicts anthropology, psychology, and sociology will be absorbed by this new science
2. It better explains human activities on the basis of genetics than other behavioral sciences on the basis of culture and learning
3. Wilson believes all social behavior is subject to processes of evolution that affect species' physical characteristics
4. Critics of sociobiology: **Bock**, 1981; **Lewontin, Rose,** and **Kamin,** 1984

SOCIAL STRUCTURE

What it is; what it is made up of; its various forms; theoretical perspectives

COMPONENTS
1. **Status**: Position within social system
   a. **Ascribed**: Characteristics over which there is little or no control (e.g. age, sex, race)
   b. **Achieved**: Characteristics which involve personal choice and achievement (e.g. job, educational level)
   c. **Status set**: Collection of all statuses (e.g. student, child, sibling, etc.)
2. **Role**: Behaviors or norms attached to specific status
3. **Role conflict**: Competition between different roles (e.g. study for exam or go to beach)
4. **Role strain**: Difficulty in adjusting to competing demands (e.g. working mothers)

GROUPS
1. **Primary group**: Small, intimate, enduring groups (e.g. family, peer group)
2. **Secondary group**: Lack of emotional bonding or sharing of common values and endurance (e.g. occupational roles)
3. **Ingroups**: Person belongs, sense of identity
4. **Outgroups**: Person does not belong, no sense of loyalty
5. **Reference groups**: Belonging to a non-important group
   a. **Normative function**: Define appropriate behavior
   b. **Comparative function**: Provide model to imitate
   c. **Audience function**: Evaluate person's behavior
6. **Social categories/Social aggregates**: People who share a common characteristic, similar status, or the same situation
7. **Organizations**
   a. Type of group that is specifically created to carry out a particular task
   b. Formal structure through which it accomplishes tasks

HOW GROUPS ARE FORMED
1. **Proximity**: Geographical closeness influences involvement
2. **Similarity**: Common ground between individuals

GROUP NORMS
1. Emerge through group interaction
2. **Sherif** (1966), perceptual test of light movement

GROUP STRUCTURE
1. **Statuses/roles**: Groups have interlocking statuses with corresponding roles
2. **Status hierarchies**: Statuses not always equal
3. **Boundaries**: Mark off members from nonmembers

GROUP PROCESSES
1. **Communication**: Members communicate information
2. **Conflict: Letha/Scanzoni** (1976), three forms
   a. Zero-sum/mixed motive
   b. Personality-based/situational
   c. Basic/nonbasic
3. **Cohesiveness**: Degree members bound to each other

POWER OF GROUP
1. **Conformity: Solomon Asch & Muzafer Sherif** experiments show a willingness to conform to group
2. **Suicide: Emile Durkheim**
   a. **Egoistic suicide**: Limited connections to group
   b. **Altruistic suicide**: Strong attachments to group (e.g. Waco, Texas suicides)
   c. **Anomic suicide**: Uncertain of which group to belong to (occurs during rapid social change)

INSTITUTIONS: Societies develop stable and reasonably consistent cultural and structural configurations to resolve recurrent problems
1. **Functionalist view**: Most societies have five major institutions (see INSTITUTIONS block for outline): Economy, Education, Family, Politics, Religion
2. Characteristics of Institutions
   a. Resist change
   b. Interdependent
3. **The Community**: A social group sharing identity, structured pattern of interaction, and geographical territory

FORMAL ORGANIZATIONS

BUREAUCRACY
1. Based on rationality and efficiency
2. **Max Weber's Model of Bureaucracy**
   a. Division of labor-specialization
   b. Hierarchy of authority-centralization
   c. Rules and regulations
   d. Impersonal relationships among workers and with clients
   e. Employment decisions based on technical competence

OLIGARCHY
1. Only a few top are in charge
2. **Robert Michels' Iron Law of Oligarchy**
   a. Democracy is antithetical to bureaucracy
   b. People at top of organization increase their power
   c. People at top become more interested in maintaining power than in interests of organization

SOCIALIZATION

Becoming a social being; learning norms/values

CHARLES HORTON COOLEY
1. The looking-glass self
2. **Self-concept**: How we think others perceive us as
   a. More important than reality

GEORGE HERBERT MEAD
1. Each person has two sides
   a. The **"I"** represents a person's individuality

b. The **"me"** represents expectations and attitudes of others
2. **Significant others**: Important role in development of "me" (e.g. parents)
3. **Generalized others**: Larger community or society

DEVIANCE

Behavior contrary to dominant norms of society

BIOLOGICAL EXPLANATIONS
[Have been discredited]
1. **William Sheldon's** body types
   a. **Endomorphic**: Soft and fat
   b. **Ectomorphic**: Thin and fragile
   c. **Mesomorphic**: Muscular and most prone to crime
2. **Extra Y chromosome theory**: Criminals have an XYY chromosome makeup rather than XY makeup

PSYCHOLOGICAL EXPLANATIONS
1. Criminals and deviants are morally inferior and suffer from keen personality deficiencies
2. Neglects the fact that most criminals are "normal" people

SOCIOLOGICAL EXPLANATIONS
1. **Robert K. Merton: Strain Theory or Theory of Opportunity Structures**
   a. Importance of financial success
   b. Not everyone has equal opportunity to achieve success
   c. This strain creates deviant behavior
2. **Edwin H. Sutherland: Differential association**; criminal behavior learned through interaction
3. **Labeling theory**
   a. No act is inherently deviant
   b. Deviance results from labeling specific act or person
   c. **Primary deviance**: Original deviant act
   d. **Secondary deviance**: Develops as result of labeling

CRIME
1. Acts contrary to legal code or laws
2. Types of crimes
   a. Against persons
      i. Violent crimes (rape, homicide, assault)
      ii. Unevenly distributed in U.S. among young, urban, poor racial minorities
   b. Against property
      i. e.g. theft including white collar crime, drug trafficking; corporate crime, such as pollution
   c. Against morality - victimless crimes (illegal gambling, prostitution)

DEMOGRAPHY

BASIC CONCEPTS

COMPOSITION OF POPULATION

CRUDE BIRTH RATE
• Number of live births per 1,000
FERTILITY RATE
• Number of live births per 1,000 women 15 to 44
CRUDE DEATH RATE (MORTALITY RATE)
• Number of deaths per 1,000
INFANT MORTALITY RATE
• Number of deaths per 1,000 live births under one year
MIGRATION
• Movement into or out of area
• Net migration rate - difference between number entering (immigrants) and leaving (emigrants) an area per 1,000

POPULATION CHANGES

THOMAS ROBERT MALTHUS (1766-1834)
1. Population will increase faster than food supply
2. Agricultural production increases arithmetically
3. Population growth increases geometrically (1-2-4-8-16-32)
4. Neglected use of technological advances to increase agriculture and decrease birthrate

KARL MARX (1818-1883)
1. Increased population is not critical problem
2. Capitalism and its reliance on a continual supply of workers creates a problem
3. The more workers, the lower wages and more unpleasant working conditions

DEMOGRAPHIC TRANSITION THEORY
1. Three stages of population growth for all societies
   a. **Low growth**: High birth rate and high death rate
   b. **Rapid growth**: High birth rate and low death rate
   c. **Stable growth**: Low birth rate and low death rate

SIGMUND FREUD
1. **Id**: Basic drives (e.g. sex, food)
2. **Superego**: Societies' expectations; censors the id
3. **Ego**: Individuality among us; mediates between id and superego

AGENTS OF SOCIALIZATION
1. Family
2. Schools
3. Peer group
4. Media

SOCIAL INEQUALITY

SOCIAL STRATIFICATION

UNEQUAL DISTRIBUTION OF POWER, PRIVILEGE & PRESTIGE
Ranking based on society's value

FUNCTIONALISM
1. Inequality is inevitable and desirable
2. Positions in society are ranked by order of importance
3. Important positions in society require more training and should receive more rewards
4. Leads to a meritocracy based on ability

CONFLICTS
1. Inequality results from power groups dominating other groups
2. Inequality impedes societal progress
3. Those in power repress powerless to maintain status quo
4. Positions are important so long as those in power deem them significant

DIMENSIONS OF SOCIAL STRATIFICATION
1. **Power**: Ability to direct someone else's behavior
2. **Prestige**: Honor or respect
3. **Privilege**: Income, wealth or property

SOCIAL CLASS

Based on education, income and occupation
UPPER CLASS
• Often inherited wealth; corporate ownership; elite education: 3-5% of the U.S.
UPPER MIDDLE CLASS
• Earned, salaried income; professionals; extensive education: 10-15% of the U.S.
LOWER MIDDLE CLASS
• Median income for U.S.; white collar sales and clerical; some college: 33% of the U.S.
WORKING CLASS
• Hourly wage; blue collar laborers; high school: 33% of the U.S.
LOWER CLASS
• Very low income, if at all; unskilled or unemployed; semi-illiterate: 20% of the U.S.
POVERTY
• 13% of the U.S. lives below poverty line
• **Feminization of poverty**: Increasingly, women disproportionate among poor

RACE

Physical characteristics
ETHNIC GROUPS
• Distinct cultural identity usually based on race, religion or national origin

INTERACTION BETWEEN MAJORITY & MINORITY
1. **Assimilation**: Accept minority into dominant culture; "melting pot"
2. **Pluralism**: Two groups remain distinct but equal
   3. **Acculturation**: Minority accepts dominant culture but still experiences segregation
   4. **Segregation**: Separation of minority from dominant culture
   5. **Expulsion**: Forcing minority to leave area
6. **Genocide**: Systematic killing of one racial and/or ethnic group

OBSTACLES TO INTEGRATION
1. **Prejudice**: Prejudging according to race or ethnic group

---

2. **Stereotype**: Set of characteristics define entire group
3. **Discrimination**: Treating groups of people unequally
   • **Institutionalized discrimination**: Patterns of discrimination part of social structure (e.g. school segregation based on residential boundaries)

GENDER INEQUALITY

Unequal power and rewards allocated to women
SEX
• Biological differences
GENDER
• Social differences based on definitions of masculinity and femininity

SYSTEMS OF GENDER INEQUALITY
1. Family - children taught gender-specific behaviors at home
2. School - curriculum, textbooks and teachers' behavior reinforce sex-role stereotyping and provide preferential treatment to boys
3. Work - women earn less than men and often encounter a "glass ceiling," whereby they are denied entry to highest levels
4. Politics - most gains for women politicians at local level

INSTITUTIONS

COLLECTION OF NORMS, ROLES & VALUES INTO A PATTERNED OR ORGANIZED WAY OF LIVING

THE ECONOMY

Distribution of goods/services

SOCIALISM: Means of production collectively owned and regulated by government
CAPITALISM
1. Private ownership of production and open competition between organizations
2. Economic inequality - large wealthy and poor class, shrinking percentage in middle class
3. 5% unemployment is considered acceptable
4. Concentration of power
   a. **Iron Law of Oligarchy**: Those in power work to maintain their power and control - when a few rule the many
   b. **Shared monopolies**: A few firms control over half market share (e.g. photography equipment [Kodak®, Polaroid®, Fuji®])
   c. **Interlocking directorships**: Members of one board of directors of a corporation sit on boards of other corporations
   d. **Multinational corporations**: International branches
COMMUNISM: Evolution of socialism into a society of economic, political and social equality
DEMOCRATIC SOCIALISM: Elements of both market and centrally controlled economy reduce social inequalities
CHANGES IN THE ECONOMY
1. Rise in global markets
   a. Decision-making at headquarters
   b. Neglect of local organizations
2. Shift from manufacturing to service
   a. Lower-paying jobs
   b. Decline of labor union strength
ECONOMIC ORDER
1. **Preindustrial order**: Economics dependent on hunting/gathering or agriculture
2. **Industrial revolution**: Cottage industry (home-produced goods) replaced by the factory
3. **Postindustrial society**: Production of information and services instead of material goods
4. Sectors of modern economy
   a. **Primary**: Take/generate resources naturally
   b. **Secondary**: Manufactured goods from primary sector
   c. **Tertiary**: Provides services instead of goods
5. Dual economy
   a. **Core sector**: Contains large economic organizations
   b. **Peripheral sector**: Small firms in one region
   c. **State sector**: Governmental agencies/companies

POLITICS

Allocation of power and authority

AUTHORITY (MAX WEBER)
1. **Traditional authority**: Historical precedent and customs (e.g. royalty)
2. **Charismatic authority**: Extraordinary personal power (e.g. **Fidel Castro**)
3. **Legal**: Based on laws (e.g. U.S. President)

POWER
1. **Legitimate power**: Power used by proper authority
2. **Illegitimate power**: Power that depends on coercion

TYPES OF POLITICAL SYSTEMS
1. **Autocracy or authoritarian state**: Power resides in one person or elite group
2. **Totalitarianism**: One group or political party maintains control
3. **Democracy**: Citizens are represented in political process

THE STATE
1. Functionalist perspective
   a. Enforcement of norms
   b. Regulation of conflict
   c. Planning and coordination
   d. Conducting relations with other societies
2. Conflict perspective
   a. **Class conflict and state**: State not a neutral arbiter
   b. **State coercion**: Defense of ruling class interests

STRUCTURE OF POWER IN U.S.
1. The **elitist** perspective
   a. **C. Wright Mills**
   b. **Three important sectors**: Executive branch of government, corporations and the military
   c. Leaders share similar outlook and vision of world order
2. The **pluralist** model
   a. Different groups compete for power, with no single group dominating for very long
   b. Political action committees (PACS) represent special interest groups to politicians
   c. Each interest group represents a veto group, insuring that no one group will dominate

EDUCATION

Teaching values and skills

FUNCTIONALIST VIEW
1. Transmission of culture - socialization
2. Prepares for adult roles through occupational training – social integration
3. Pathway into structure of society – social placement
4. Increases number of educated individuals in society – cultural innovation
5. Latent functions – unintended consequences of education, e.g. life-long relationships develop

CONFLICT THEORY VIEW
1. Perpetuation of social inequality
2. **Social control**: Education meets need of capitalist society, Bowles and Gintis (1976)
3. **Credentialism**: Education a screening process for the elite
4. **Testing controversy**: Intelligence/aptitude tests to measure ability
5. Hidden curriculum
   a. Respect for authority
   b. Need to follow rules
   c. Importance of competition
6. Development of contrary student subculture
7. **Tracking**: Grouping students according to ability perpetuates social class status quo

VEHICLE TO UPWARD MOBILITY
1. Family's social class greatest predictor of academic success due to motivational norms
2. Quality of teachers and equipment have greatest impact in poorer school where quality is often substandard
3. Peer group influence can be negative - students of similar backgrounds form peer group, thus reinforcing negative or positive behavior
4. Organizational characteristics - school climate (academic, vocational, athletic) will influence academic achievement
   a. Teacher's attitudes work against lower-class students
      i. Value conflict between teachers and students

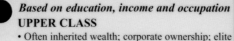